You're NEVER too Old to LAUGH

A laugh-out-loud collection of cartoons, quotes, jokes, and trivia on growing older

Ed Fischer

⚏ **Meadowbrook Press**

Distributed by Simon & Schuster
New York

Fischer, Ed.
You're Never too Old to Laugh
ISBN-13: 978-0-88166-576-5 (Meadowbrook Press)
ISBN-13: 978-1-451-67049-3 (Simon & Schuster)
1. Aging--Caricatures and cartoons.
2. Old age--Caricatures and cartoons.
3. American wit and humor, Pictorial.

Cover Art and Interior Cartoons: Ed Fischer

Published by
Meadowbrook Press
6110 Blue Circle Drive, Suite 237
Minnetonka, Minnesota 55343

www.meadowbrookpress.com

BOOK TRADE DISTRIBUTION by
Simon and Schuster
a division of Simon and Schuster, Inc.
1230 Avenue of the Americas
New York, New York 10020

16 15 14 13 12   15 14 13 12 11 10 9 8 7 6 5 4

Printed in the United States of America

WELCOME TO THE NEW "OLD".

Gone are the days of retiring to a rocking chair. Today, it's the start of a fresh new life... a time to rock! Golf, camping with the grandkids, travel, adventure, laughter, and maybe a grander appreciation of beauty and what's important. Start here with the wit and wisdom of the ages and the laughter you need to rise above the maladies that just come naturally with getting older.

Be a little quirky. It's allowed.

It's time for you to be the new you!

ED FISCHER

To Vernon and Donna

I used to dread
getting older because
I thought I would not
be able to do all the
things I wanted to
do, but now that I am
older, I find that
I don't <u>want</u> to
do them.

-Nancy Astor

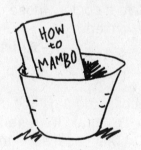

HAPPINESS IS:
Hearing your proctologist say,
"You can straighten up now."
– George Burns

~

Patient: Doc, every time I drink coffee,
I get a stabbing sensation in my eye.
Doctor: Next time, take the spoon out
of the cup.
– Anonymous

~

Never go to a doctor whose office
plants have died.
– Erma Bombeck

~

Doctor: I can't do anything about your
condition. I'm afraid it's hereditary.
Patient: In that case, send the bill to
my parents.
– Joe Claro

Everytime
I move,
I
leak.
ED FISCHER

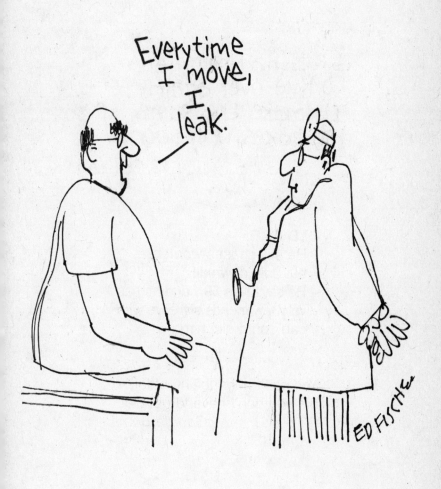

If I had my life
to live over again
I'd make the same
mistakes, only sooner.

-Tallulah Bankhead

OLD AGE:
- He still chases women...
  but only downhill.
- He says he's 59...and he has
  very few friends still alive who
  can contradict him.

You can't help getting older,
but you don't have to get old.
— *George Burns*

I'm worried about you, Dad- you don't seem to have that ol' vim and vigor....
ED FISCHER

You're getting old when you feel on Saturday night what you used to feel on Monday morning.

You know you're getting old when...

Your head makes promises your body can't possibly keep.

A 55-year-old widow went out on a blind date with a 65-year-old man. Returning to her daughter's house around 10:30, she seemed quiet and upset. "What happened?" asked the daughter. "I had to slap his face three times." "You mean...?" began her daughter. "Yes," she answered, "he fell asleep three times!"

1
What will it be this morning- sex or oatmeal?
2
Well?
3
I'm thinking about it.
ED FISCHER

The future just isn't what it used to be.

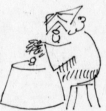

Nostalgia...

The ability to remember yesterday's prices while forgetting yesterday's wages.

– Los Angeles Times Syndicate

Old Timer...

Someone who can remember when bacon, eggs and sunshine were good for us.

– Treasury of Medical Humor, *edited by James E. Myers*

the economy being what it is, we've had to make a few changes in your retirement plan...
Financial Planner
BurgerBusters
would you like fries - with that?
Burger Busters
©ED FISCHER

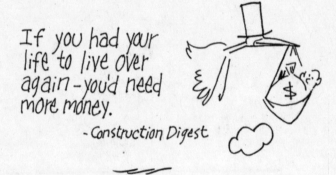

If you had your life to live over again - you'd need more money.

- Construction Digest

Joe was the type who loved to talk about the good old days. At a movie, he told the girl who handed him his five-dollar ticket, "I can remember when a movie ticket was only fifteen cents." "You're really going to enjoy this movie then, sir," said the ticket girl. "We have sound now."

It was a major operation-
they removed my savings
account... my car..
my house...
ED FISCHER

First you forget names,
then you forget faces,
then you forget to pull up your zipper,
then you forget to pull your zipper
                              down!
— Leo Rosenberg

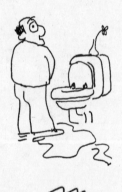

Q: Is it common for 50-year-olds
to have problems with short-term
memory storage?
A: Storing memory is not a problem.
Retrieving it is a problem.

— P. D. Witte

CLASS OF '68
REUNION
I can't believe we dated...
ED FISCHER

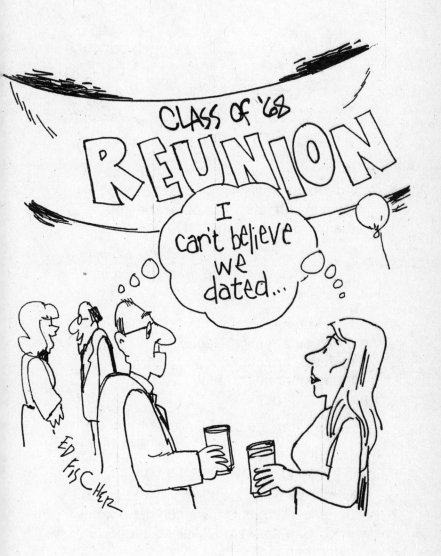

Youth is a gift of nature, but age is a work of art.
— Garson Kanin

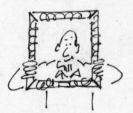

～

An archaeologist is the best husband a woman can have. The older she gets, the more he is interested in her.

*– Agatha Christie
(who married an archaeologist)*

～

First you are young;
then you are middle-aged;
then you are old;
then you are wonderful.

*– Lady Diana Cooper
(from the book* Gallimaufry to Go*,
by J. Bryan, III)*

～

Someone asked the 80-year-old countess of Essex, "When is a woman done with sex?" She answered, "Ask someone older than me."

Ever since their TV broke...
ED FISCHER

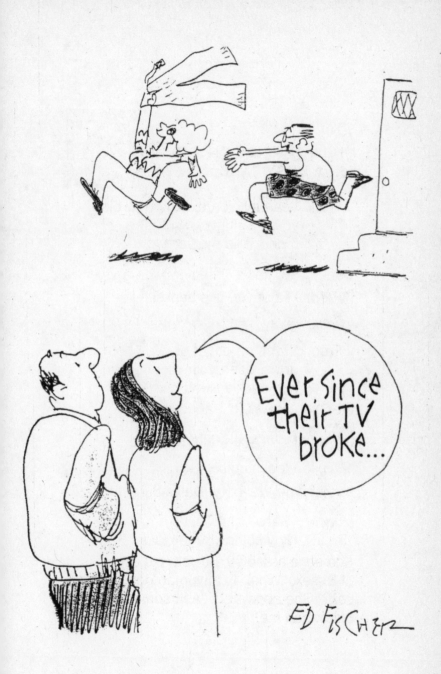

NEW FRIENDS ON A BENCH
IN A BUSY PARK...

Fred: I can tell you exactly how old you are right down to the month and the year.

Jack: Get outta here.

Fred: I'll bet you five bucks.

Jack: Okay.

Fred: Stand on one leg, raise both arms, open your mouth wide, and cackle like a chicken.

Jack: What?

Fred: Do it. I can tell from that.

Jack: I feel stupid.

Fred: You were 63 last March.

Jack: That's right! That's amazing! How could you tell I was 63 last March?

Fred: You told me yesterday.

Feed the birds often?
ED FISCHER

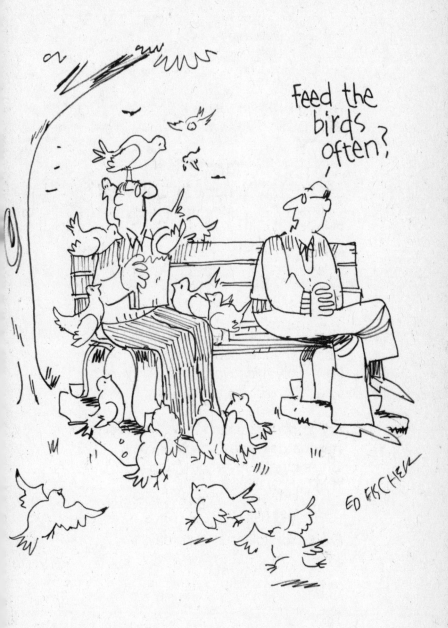

I like long walks,
especially when they are
taken by people who
annoy me.
— Fred Allen

∿

If you have nothing pleasant to say
about anyone, come and sit by me.
— *Alice Roosevelt Longworth*

∿

My grandmother started walking five
miles a day when she was sixty.
She's ninety-seven now and we
don't know where she is.
— *Ellen DeGeneres*

What day is it?
monday
what year is it?
Oboy!
ED FISCHER

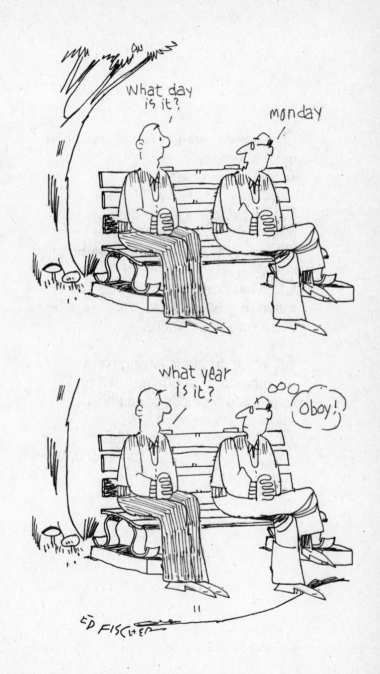

Q: How do retired executives spend most afternoons?
A: Power napping.

Q: As people age, do they sleep more soundly?
A: Yes, but usually in the afternoon.

Q: What does "afternoon delight" mean to a 50-year-old?
A: A nap after lunch.

Q: What do the following have in common for a 60-year-old: an opera, a neighbor's slide show, and the Tunnel of Love?
A: All are nap opportunities.

– P. D. Witte

Whoops-
yes-this is the
time Joe usually
takes his nap...
Z z z z z
ED FISCHER

Retire? What could I retire to?
What else am I going to play with?

– Duke Ellington

Q: Why is it no longer common to give a retiree a watch?
A: It finally dawned on personnel departments that retired folks don't care what time it is.

Q: What's the best indication a retiree has done his job well?
A: It's taken two people and a computer program to replace him.

Q: I hate to admit it, but some days I miss work. What can I do?
A: Listen to rush-hour traffic reports.

– Bill Dodds

Senior Citizen CENTER
How much time do you have for activities?
About 20 years...
art classes
Dance
ED FISCHER

I went on a diet. Had to go on two diets at the same time 'cause one diet wasn't giving me enough food!

— Barry Marter

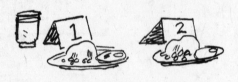

Happiness is good health and a bad memory.

– *Ingrid Bergman*

Billie says when she was young it was "Look, but don't touch." Now she says it's "Touch, but don't look."

IT'S GREAT TO BE OLD BECAUSE:
You don't have to diet anymore.
You've tried all the diets. They obviously don't work, or you'd already be thin.
Are you suddenly going to be buff after years of being a blob?
Look around. You look like everyone else your age—skinny legs, lumpy thighs, flabby arms, saggy butt.
Dieting isn't for people who like to eat.

– *Jim Dale*

you're not gaining weight, you have my pants on...
ED FISCHER

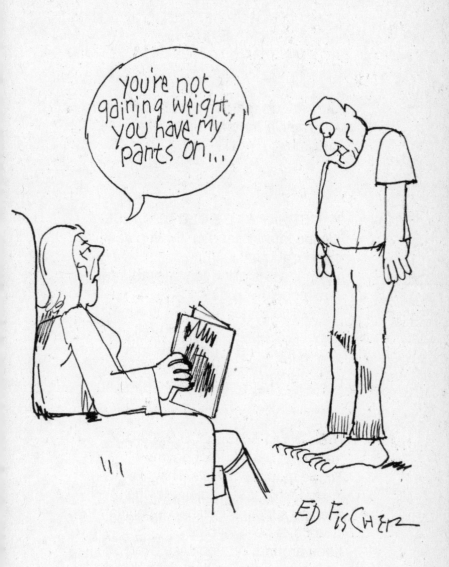

Q: Why do retirees count pennies?
A: They're the only ones who have the time.

– Bill Dodds

IT'S GREAT TO BE OLD BECAUSE:

It's too late to get rich. So you can relax about it.

Even if you started this minute, how rich could you get?

Why save up for a rainy day when you already have an umbrella and galoshes and a good raincoat?

Hey, these aren't the prime earning years. They're the prime spending years. You're doing your part for the economy.

Why invest for old age when you're already old?

Hey, maybe you can still make a fortune overnight. There's only one way to find out: Go to sleep.

– Jim Dale

Irma likes to keep the house on the cool side...
ED FISCHER

You're old enough to be a grandma if...

Someone calls you "spry."

The things you talk about to your doctor take more than one sheet of paper.

After becoming a grandparent, you need reality therapy for grandmas who think their grandchildren are perfect.

∿

You're officially old when people no longer say, "Gee, you don't look old enough to be a grandparent!"

∿

Thanksgiving comes after Christmas for those grandparents who entertain the whole family on Christmas Day.

∿

A Norwegian grandma's favorite dinner-time saying: "*Eat, drink, and be quiet!*"

Don't you like it?
I've already had four helpings.
ED FISCHER

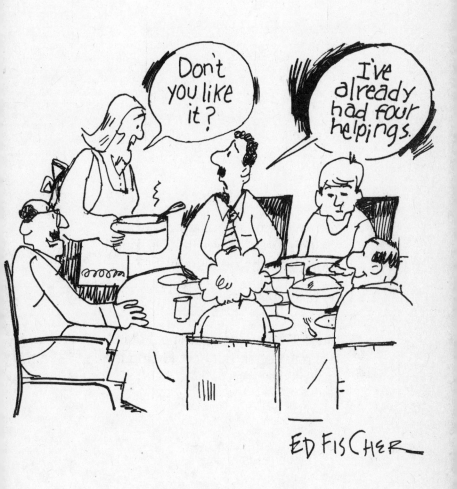

Of course Americans trust in God. You can tell the way they drive.

You know you're getting old when "getting lucky" means you've found your car in the parking lot.
                                    – Bruce Lansky

I tried Flintstones vitamins. I didn't feel any better, but I could stop the car with my feet.
                                    – Joan St. Onge

IF YOU REMEMBER
THE BURMA SHAVE SIGN
CHANCES ARE
YOU'RE OVER 59
ED FISCHER

You know someone's had too much coffee when they answer a question before you've asked it.

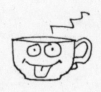

~

Kenny, in his late fifties, noticed that senior citizens get free coffee at a local cafe. He asked, "How old do you have to be to be a senior citizen?" The waiter looked at him for a few seconds and without saying a word, poured him a cup of coffee.

~

Q: What's the best way to describe retirement?
A: The coffee break that never ends.

– Bill Dodds

~

Q: What is the most common question that 50-year-olds ask at restaurants?
A: "Are you sure that's decaffeinated coffee?"

– P. D. Witte

__________ __________ __________

Sip and Gossip
cafe
Today's special
Irma Swartz
ED FISCHER

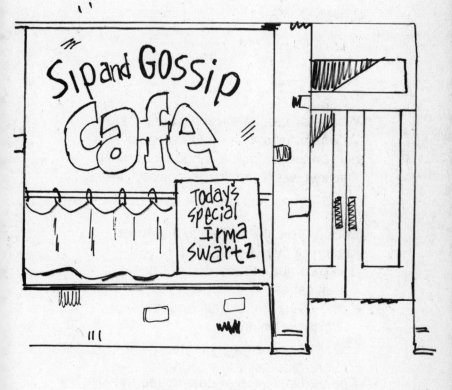

I like TV better than the movies – it's not so far to the bathroom.

– Cecil B. DeMille

～

What a difference a few decades make. When TV first came on the scene, it was only on the air for a few hours…and half that time was taken up with cowboy chases.

～

Let's hear it for the things that have made our lives better…
…like company-recorded phone messages.
…like 100 TV channels and nothing worth watching!

～

The early bird never gets to see the 10 o'clock news.

Now for the good news... the news is over.
ED FISCHER

Wrinkles are hereditary.
You get them
from your kids!
— Erma Bombeck

~

Ever notice that you have to get
old before people start saying how
young you look?
— Joey Adams

~

I have everything I had twenty years
ago, only it's all a little bit lower.
— Gypsy Rose Lee

~

I don't know how you feel about old
age, but in my case I didn't even see
it coming. It hit me from the rear.
— Phyllis Diller

He has to stop to pee more than I do...
ED FISCHER

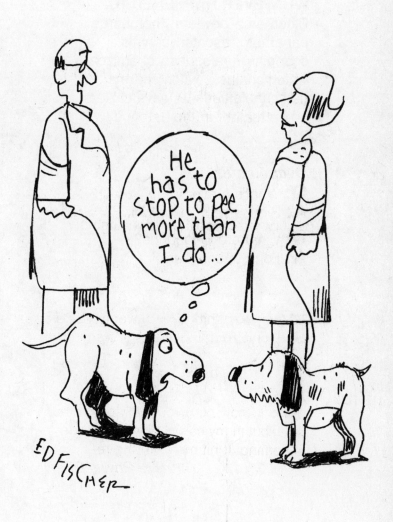

WHATEVER HAPPENED TO...
Bloomers...bowlers...homburgs...
panamas...ascots...cravats...
scarfpins...galoshes...chemises...
watch chains...watch charms...
detachable cuffs...sleeve garters...
and a feather in the hatband?

Over 50 quiz...
Q: What's a middy?
A: Blouse with sailor look.

Q: What are long johns?
A: Long underwear.

60-year-old Martha's fashion style consists of buying anything that doesn't itch.

She shopped 'til she dropped.
women's wear
ED FISCHER

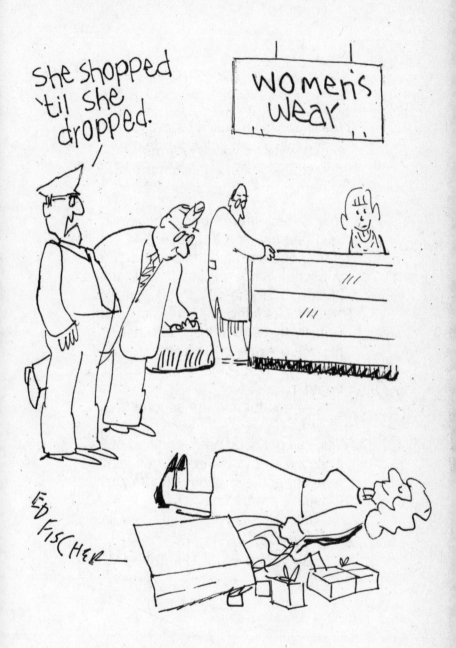

It really doesn't matter if there's life after
death if there isn't golf after death.

— *Bruce Lansky*

"Do you think there's golf in heaven?"
  said one old man to another.
"I sure hope so," said the second. "I tell
  you what. Whoever dies first will come
  back and tell the other."
Three weeks later, the first fellow died.
  Shortly thereafter, his friend heard
  his voice as he lay in bed.
"Bill, I've come back to tell you about
  heaven."
"Is there golf there?" the second man
  asked.
"Well, I've got good news and bad news.
  The good news is there is golf in
  heaven, and everybody shoots par."
"So what's the bad news?"
"The bad news is you've got a tee time
  next Tuesday."

— *Lewis Grizzard*

This going to take long?... I'm supposed to tee off soon...
MARRIAGE COUNSELOR
ED FISCHER

Every day, I eat
from the four basic
food groups: Milk
chocolate, dark chocolate,
White chocolate, and
cocoa.

—Debra Tracy

I hate skinny women, especially when
they say things like, "Sometimes I forget
to eat." Now, I've forgotten my mother's
maiden name… I've forgotten my car
keys… but you've got to be a special
kind of stupid to forget to eat.

— *Marsha Warfield*

Old people shouldn't eat health food.
They need all the preservatives they
can get.

— *Anonymous*

weight and fortune
LIFE IS SHORT.
PIG OUT.
ED FISCHER

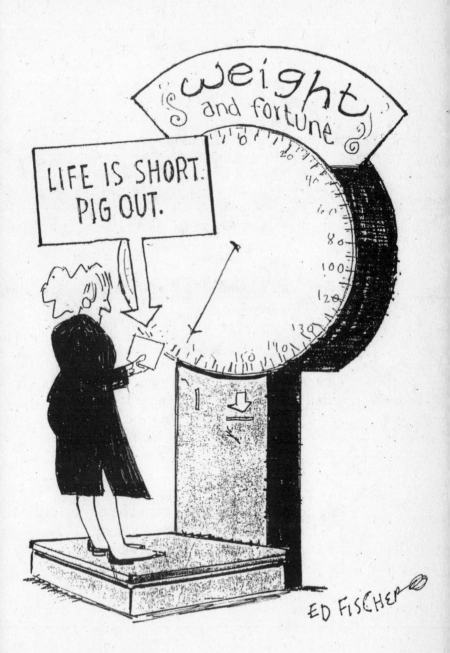

While governor of New York, Teddy Roosevelt held press conferences after running up the seventy-seven steps of the state capitol in Albany. Any reporter who still had the breath to ask a question was given an answer.

Puff Puff?

Press

I don't jog. It makes the ice jump right out of my glass.

— *Martin Mull*

I joined a health club last year, spent about 400 bucks. Haven't lost a pound. Apparently you have to show up.

— *Rich Ceisler*

I try to spend an hour at the club every day now. That includes a ten-minute whirlpool, ten-minute sauna, and forty minutes circling the parking lot looking for a space near the door.

— *Susan Vass*

I'm floating downstream...
Northside Fitness
Rowing Machine
ED FISCHER

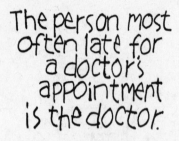

The person most often late for a doctor's appointment is the doctor.

~~

When you think that the medical world knows everything, remember, ketchup was once sold as medicine.
— Nantucket Inquirer and Mirror

~~

My doctor put his hand on my wallet and asked me to cough.

~~

The instructions read, "Take one pill, three times a day." How am I supposed to do that? Tie a string to it?
— Anonymous

~~

The doctor handed her overweight patient a bottle of pills. "Don't take these pills," she said. "Spill them on the floor and pick them up one by one."
— Joe Claro

Pharmacy
You're going to need this when you get the bill...
ED FISCHER

Two can live as cheaply as one, but for only half as long.

～

Visiting the Social Security office for the first time is like the first day of school when you were a child. You feel like you don't belong there, but there isn't much you can do about it.

– Pearl Swiggum

～

I'm proud to be paying taxes in the United States. The only thing is – I could be just as proud for half the money.

– Arthur Godfrey

retirement Party
Gee... uh, thanks
Old Fart
ED FISCHER

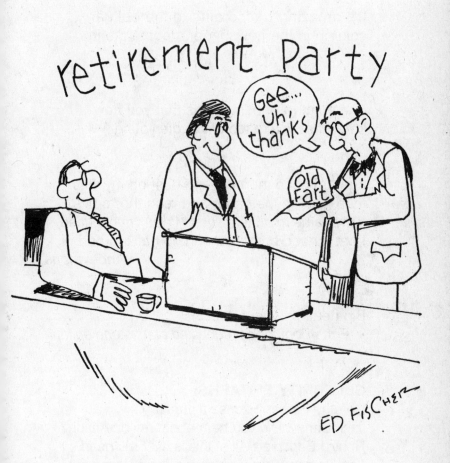

It's amazing...according to the obituary column in the newspaper, people die in alphabetical order.

∿

The comfort of being 59 is that you now know that you're too old to die young.

∿

I get up each morning and dust off my wits,
then pick up the paper and read the "o-bits."
If my name isn't there, then I know I'm not dead.
I eat a good breakfast and go back to bed.

— *Anonymous*

∿

Big deal! I'm used to dust.
— *Erma Bombeck's requested gravestone epitaph*

∿

CELEBRITY EPITAPHS:
Dorothy Parker: Excuse my dust.
Jack Benny: Did you hear about my operation?
Robert Benchley: All of this is over my head.
Leo Rosten: This is much too deep for me.

— *Anonymous*

ED FISCHER
OUT
INTENSIVE CARE
PAY ↑
HOSPITAL BILL HERE

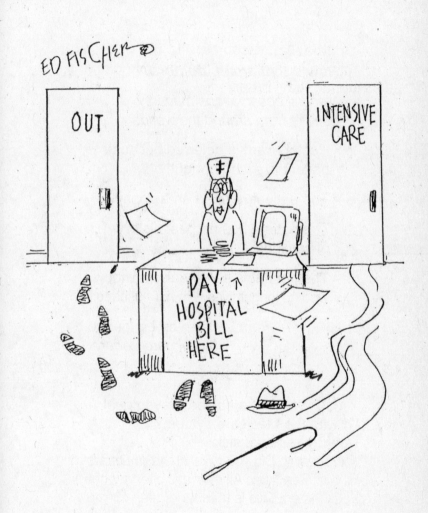

How's that again, doctor...?

Medical observations made by doctors from around the world:

- Rectal exam is deferred because patient is sitting upright.

- The patient refused an autopsy.

- The patient has no past history of suicides.

- The patient is a 79-year-old widow who no longer lives with her husband.

> – *From* Lederer on Language
> *by Richard Lederer*

~

Q: What's the easiest way to deal with the Medicare system?
A: Never get sick.

> – *Bill Dodds*

Maybe we could put our knitting down until the examination is over...
ED FISCHER

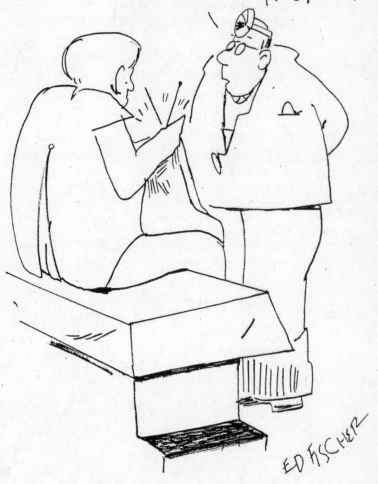

Book title by Lois Wyse:
Grandchildren are so much fun,
I should have had them first.

~~

One 68-year-old:
   "Have I shown you pictures
   of my grandchildren?"
His 70-year-old friend:
   "You haven't, and I've been
   meaning to thank you."

~~

You feel completely comfortable
entrusting your baby to [them] for
long periods, which is why most
grandparents flee to Florida at
the earliest opportunity.
                    – Dave Barry

Can you say something to Grandma? Can you say 'Grandma'?
Babysitter!
ED FISCHER

YOU KNOW YOU'RE GETTING OLDER WHEN...

…The gleam in your eye is from the sun hitting your bifocals.

…You feel like the morning after the night before, except you haven't been anywhere.

…You decide to procrastinate, but then never get around to it.

…You look forward to a dull evening.

…You sit in a rocking chair but can't get it going.

…A fortuneteller offers to read your face.

…Dialing long distance wears you out.

…You look forward to calls from telemarketers.

No, I'm not interested in aluminum siding... but say - how's the weather in Phoenix... boy, wish I could show you pictures of my grandkids... my back went out the other day, and, know what?

ED FISCHE

One thing about being bald—it's neat.

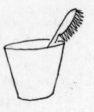

〰

A hair in the head is worth two in the brush.

– Oliver Herford

〰

Q: What do you call a 50-year-old man with no gray hair?
A: Bald.

– P. D. Witte

Hair
grower
ED FISCHER

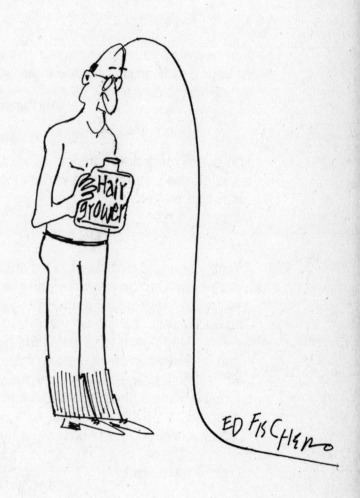

Just because your doctor has a name
for your condition doesn't mean he
knows how to cure it.

— *Anonymous*

The art of medicine consists of
amusing the patient while Nature
cures the disease.

— *Voltaire*

A ninety-year-old man went to his doctor
    and said, "Doctor, my wife—who is
    eighteen—is expecting a baby."
The doctor said, "Let me tell you a story.
    A man went hunting, but instead of his
    gun, he picked up an umbrella by mistake.
    And when a bear suddenly charged at
    him, he pointed his umbrella at the bear,
    shot, and killed it on the spot."
"Impossible. Somebody else must have
    shot that bear."
"Exactly my point."

— *Anonymous*

Thanks for asking... my back aches, I can't turn my neck, I see spots in my left eye, I have a bunion on my heel......
ED FISCHER

If you are going to try cross-country skiing, start from a small country.
— From Saturday Night Live

～

And now for your morning exercise. Ready? Up, down, up, down, up, down, up, down. And now the other eyelid.
— Fred Metcalf

～

REMEMBER WHEN...

- There was no place to go where you shouldn't?

- "Come again" was painted on the back of the "Welcome to" sign of a town?

- If you didn't know what was going on...probably nothing was?

- The only place air-conditioned was the movies?

You're supposed to do it more than once...
phew
ED FISCHER

Mee of Little Canada, Minnesota, noticed on a coupon for quilted toilet tissue that it was "100% recycled bathroom tissue." "Some things just shouldn't be recycled," says Mee.

~~

Elaine from Ely, Minnesota, tells this story: There was an explosion at a local senior citizen's center and 50 of the group died and went to Heaven. St. Peter apologized that Heaven was full and they would have to go to Hell temporarily until space opened up. After a month, an angel came to St. Peter and said: "We'd better do something about getting those seniors back up to Heaven." "Why?" asked St. Peter. "Because," the angel said, "they've held several bake sales and have raised the money to buy a large number of air conditioners."

Meeting
tonight
Garage
sale
anonymous
8:00 PM
ED FISCHER

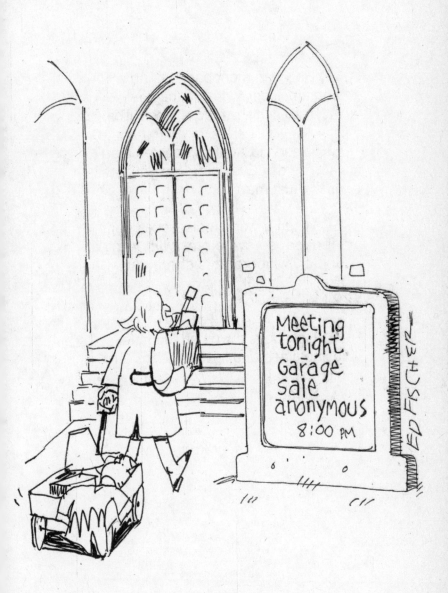

Q: How can menopause bring a woman closer to her teenagers?
A: They can share acne medication.

Q: When did Adam's troubles start?
A: The day Eve said, "Are you hot, or is it just me?"

Q: When a woman discusses her menopause symptoms with her doctor, which one is she most likely to forget?
A: Memory loss.

Q: How does a woman feel after losing sleep due to hot flashes and night sweats?
A: Steamed.

– Linda Knaus and
Kathy Kenney-Marshall

I'm having a hot flash-hope you don't mind if I turn on the fan...
ED FISCHER

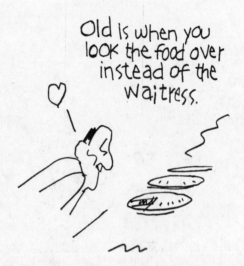

Old is when you look the food over instead of the waitress.

Q: Are there certain foods that 50-year-olds shouldn't eat?
A: Yes. Avoid any food that is spicy, salty, fried, fattening, creamy, meaty, filling, satisfying, or delicious.

– P. D. Witte

Q: Why do 60-year-olds ask to see a menu before entering a restaurant?
A: To see if the print is large enough to read.

– P. D. Witte

What do you want, old timer?
I want a waitress who doesn't call me 'old timer.'
menu
ED FISCHER

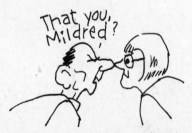

The best thing that can happen to a couple married for fifty years or more is that they both grow nearsighted together.

– Linda Fiterman

Q: Is a person's sense of hearing less acute at age 50?
A: Not at all. It's just that other people mumble more than they used to.

– P. D. Witte

Q: When do you know it's time to buy a hearing aid?
A: When the burglar alarm goes off and you check to see who's ringing the doorbell.

– P. D. Witte

I said bring bread home for supper- not bring Fred home for supper!
Fred
ED FISCHER

How is it...some 60-year-olds can polka for hours but can't bend over to pick up a gum wrapper?

∿

Whatever happened to fifty-cent pieces?

∿

The thing about getting old is everything is harder to reach than it used to be.

∿

You know you're getting old when you have to sit down to brush your teeth.

Is bending over worth a quarter?
ED FISCHETTO

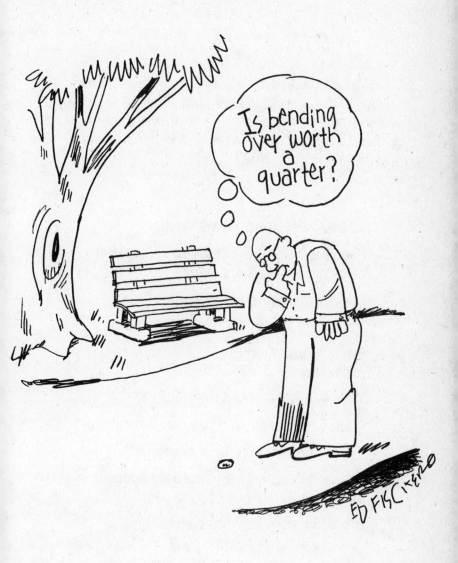

Alice was asked by a friend if she ever thinks about the hereafter. She said, "I do all the time. No matter where I am in the house, kitchen, den, upstairs, downstairs, I ask myself, 'Now, what am I here after?' "

~

THOSE WERE THE DAYS WHEN:

– People sat down to dinner and counted their blessings instead of calories.

– People who wore jeans worked.

– Dirty words in books were dots and dashes.

– Baths were taken once a week and religion every day.

– The hero only kissed the heroine.

– A job was the first thing you went steady with.

– People dressed up for church.

– A baseball game was called on account of darkness.

– Breakfast cereals were silent.

ED FISCHER
Bless the turkey—and bless the bird we are about to eat...

They say that regular naps prevent old age...especially if you take them while driving.
— *James E. Myers*

∿

I've been trying to read a book titled *How to Fight Insomnia*, but I can't seem to get interested in it. I keep falling asleep.
— *Steve Allen*

∿

I haven't been to sleep for over a year. That's why I go to bed early. One needs more rest if one doesn't sleep.
— *Evelyn Waugh*

It's time to get up.
Why?
'Cause my eyes are open.
ED FISCH

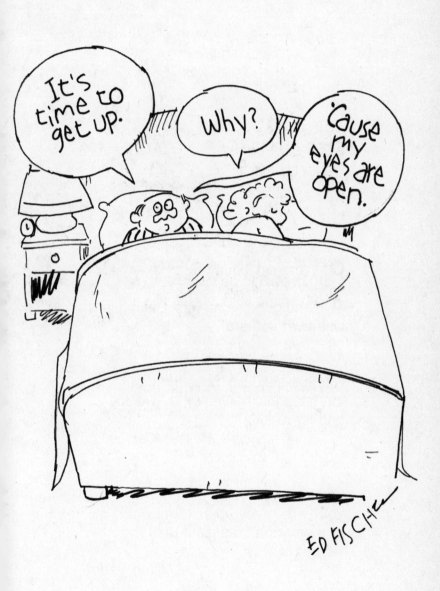

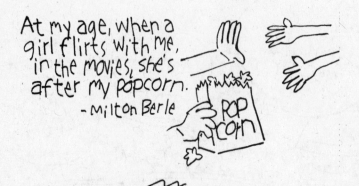

At my age, when a girl flirts with me, in the movies, she's after my popcorn.
– Milton Berle

~

Q: What did Jimmy Durante say at the end of his shows?
A: "And good night, Mrs. Calabash, wherever you are."

~

A man's sexuality goes through three stages: tri-weekly, try-weekly, and try-weakly.
– *Sydnie Meltzer Kleinhenz*

~

You know you're getting old when your wife gives up sex for Lent, and you don't realize it until the Fourth of July.

– *Milton Berle*

Does this mean you want a back rub?

ED FISCHER

IT'S GREAT TO BE OLD BECAUSE:

You don't need to run. You walk.

Nothing, absolutely nothing, is worth running for. You've run after things your whole life, and they've never been worth it.

There's always another bus. That's why it's called a bus stop.

Even if there's only one elevator, it has to come down again.

If the traffic light tells you, "Don't walk," you don't walk. The stores will still be there when you get to the other side.

– Jim Dale

You know you're getting old when the little gray-haired lady you're helping across the street is your wife.

– John Ross

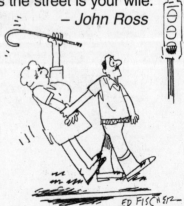

ED FISCHER

Grumpy
old men
crossing
SPEEDERS BEWARE
ED FISCHER

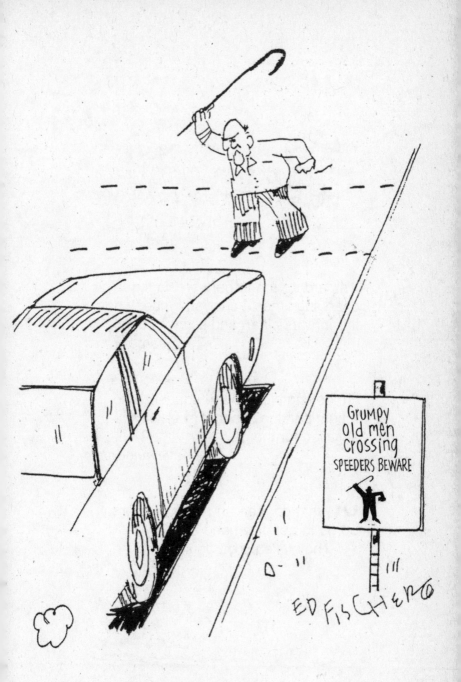

At my age, "getting a little action" means I need to take a laxative.
— Bruce Lansky

〜

It's hard for me to get used to these changing times. I can remember when the air was clean and sex was dirty.
— *George Burns*

〜

I'm getting old. When I squeeze into a tight parking space, I'm sexually satisfied for the day.
— *Rodney Dangerfield*

〜

Q: What do men and women over 50 do to get down and dirty?
A: They take up gardening.
— *P. D. Witte*

My wife still gets passionate – Unfortunately, she gets passionate about shopping...

ED FISCHER

Laugh and the world laughs
with you, snore and you
sleep alone.
                    —Anthony Burgess

~~

Why is it that the person who snores
is always the first one to fall asleep?

~~

He: I slept like a log.
She: More like a sawmill.

Mattress only SALE
ZZZZzzzz
we'll take it.
ED FISCHER

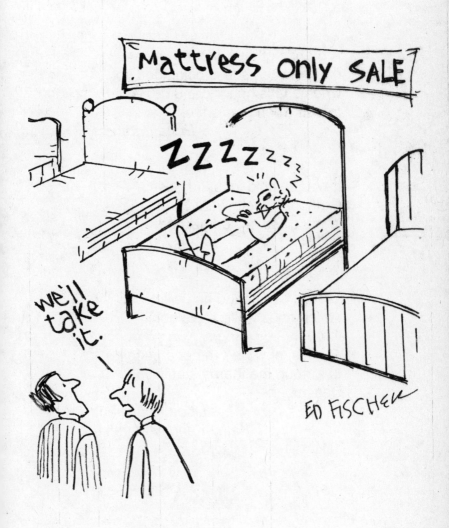

A grandmother will put a sweater
on you when she is cold, feed you
when she is hungry, and put you
to bed when she is tired.

> – *Erma Bombeck*

~~

It was so cold in their house...
Grandpa's teeth were chattering—
in the glass beside his bed!

> – *Anonymous*

~~

Q: Do a husband and wife ever
switch roles while she's going
through the change?
A: Yes, now *he's* the one begging
to turn up the thermostat in
December.

> – *Linda Knaus and*
> *Kathy Kenney-Marshall*

Cold?
ED FISCHER

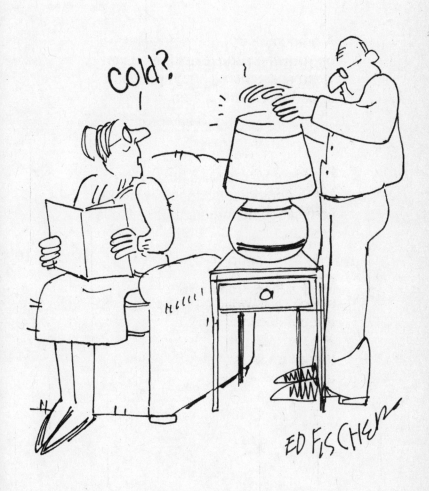

YOU'RE OLD WHEN...
...you begin to think, gee, 65 isn't so old.
...you, ah...ah...you forget what
   you were going to say next.

～

George's friend, Mike, says George
has a photographic memory. It's just
sometimes he forgets to take the lens
cap off.

～

Mary suffers from CRS:
   Can't Remember Stuff

This is my wife of 42 years... uh...
Lisa.
ED FISCHER

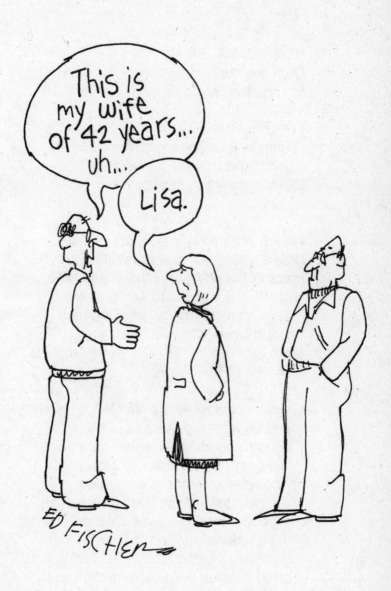

NOWADAYS...
Over the river and through the woods
to Grandmother's condo we go...

~~

You know you have a problem grandchild
when you remove him from church and
the congregation applauds.

~~

How to show off a grandchild's photos...
Before you push your cart within arm's
reach of the checker at the supermarket,
say, "Would you like to see pictures of
the grandchildren who will be eating
these groceries?"

— *Mary McBride*

~~

*Grandchildren today are handled differently
than they were in years past...*
It used to be children were spanked.
  Nowadays they're taken to a pediatrician
  who refers them to a counselor.
Kids used to get watches for their high
  school graduation. Now children wear
  them to kindergarten.
Kids used to turn off the TV so they
  could do their homework. Now they
  just record the programs on a TiVo.

How do you turn it on, grandpa...?
Official Yo-Yo
ED FISCHER

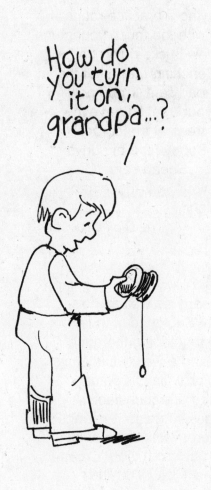

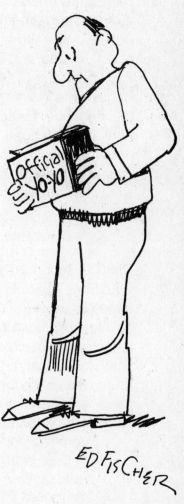

Sam Snead was playing a practice round at Augusta National with the much younger Bobby Cole (with a few bucks riding on the match, of course). Reaching the tee at the dogleg-left par-5, Snead said, "You know Bobby, when I was your age, I'd drive the ball right over those trees at the corner." Feeling challenged, Bobby hit a big drive right into the big trees. Snead said, "Of course, when I was your age, those trees were only ten feet high."

– Dick Crouser

∿

Chi Chi Rodriguez did okay on the regular PGA Tour, but not nearly as well as he's done on the over-fifty Senior Tour. In fact, he's looking forward to keeping the good times rolling by creating a Really Old Guys Tour (over eighty). "You'll play three-day tournaments, shooting one hole each day," he says. "Then the guy who can remember each of his three scores wins the money."

– Dick Crouser

ED FISCHER ©

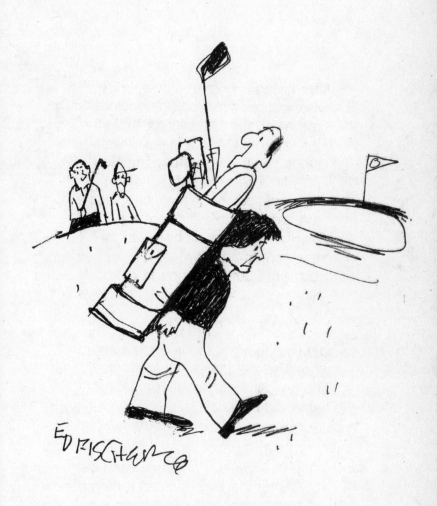

After giving a woman a complete
  medical examination, the doctor
  explained his prescription. "Take
  the green pill with a glass of water
  when you wake up. Take the blue
  pill with a glass of water after lunch.
  Then just before going to bed, take
  the red pill with a glass of water."
"Exactly what is my problem, Doctor?"
  the woman asked.
"You're not drinking enough water."
                    – *Anonymous*

Did you hear about the three men
who hijacked a truck full of Viagra?
The police are looking for a gang of
hardened criminals.
                    – *Anonymous*

DRUGS
...And take these three times a day or whenever you can get the childproof cap off....
ED FISCHER

You know you're getting
old when your wife asks
you to pull in your stomach,
and you already have.

Alf's wife was so neat, every time
he got up to go to the bathroom,
she made the bed.

Some people ask the secret of our
long marriage. We take time to go
to a restaurant two times a week.
A little candlelight, dinner, soft music,
and dancing. She goes Tuesdays;
I go Fridays.

— Henry Youngman

We've been married for 40 years...
...and he still can't find his socks.
ED FISCHER ©

Death bothers Woody Allen, because, he muses, if the soul is immortal and lives on after the body, he's afraid his clothes will not fit.

~~~

Q: When is it time to update the 50-year-old's wardrobe?
A: When trick-or-treaters wear costumes that resemble some of your casual wear.

– P. D. Witte

~~~

IT'S GREAT TO BE OLD BECAUSE:
You can wear loud shorts and knee
  socks and T-shirts that say things like,
"I'm not old…compared to a fossil."
"I'm not old. I'm…what was I saying?"

– Jim Dale

Alice!, did you submit my name for TV's 'what-not-to-wear!?
Bears
TED FISCHER

The early bird gets the worm.
The snowbird gets the heck out of town.

Flight...
Q: Remember the Spirit of St. Louis,
Enola Gay, the Flyer, the Spruce Goose,
and the Voyager? But what about the
Tingmissartog?
A: Tingmissartog was the plane Charles
and Anne Lindberg flew to the Arctic and
the Orient.

IT'S GREAT TO BE OLD BECAUSE:
You can go to Florida a lot.
You can get a discount on your airfare
  just for being old.
When you get there, you can eat early-
  bird specials.
You can complain about how hot it is to
  your friends up north who are digging
  out of a blizzard.
You can wear loud shorts and knee socks.
                                    – *Jim Dale*

AIRLINE
GATE
2A
Anywhere warm.
TICKETS
ED FISCHER

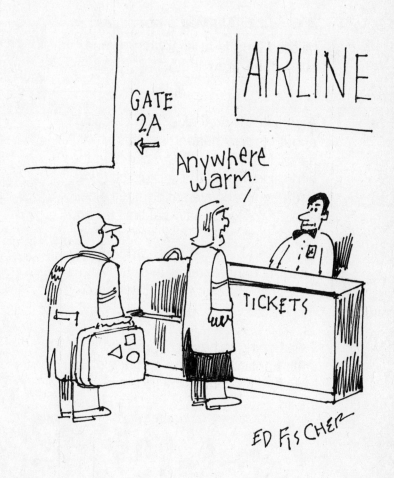

A friend of Mildred's observes:

Mildred laughs at everything since she got her new teeth.

~~

A particularly deaf elder was bragging about his new hearing aid. "It's great," he said to a friend. "I now can hear the birds singing and the crickets chirping. I can hear a conversation a full block away." "You don't say," said his friend. "What kind is it?" The proud owner consulted his wristwatch and said, "Twenty minutes after two."

– Bennett Cerf

~~

I was going to have cosmetic surgery until I noticed that the doctor's office was full of portraits by Picasso.

– Rita Rudner

but, I don't want your false teeth
ED FISCHER

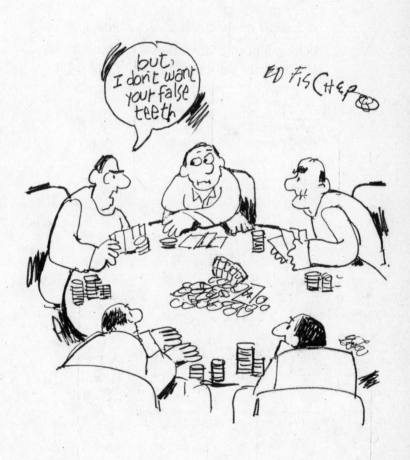

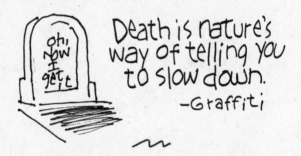

Death is nature's way of telling you to slow down.
— Graffiti

~

I prefer old age to the alternative.
— *Maurice Chevalier*

~

I much prefer being over the hill to being under it.
— *Bruce Lansky*

~

Just remember, once you're over
the hill, you begin to pick up speed.
— *Charles Schulz*

My grandpa's faster than your granpa!
ED FISCHER

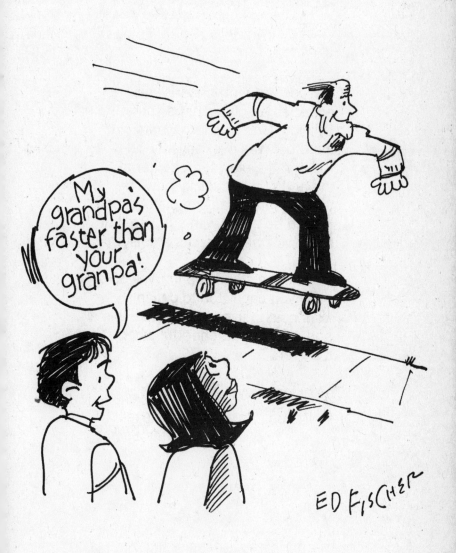

Two successful psychoanalysts
occupied an office in the same
building. One was forty years old,
the other was over seventy. They
rode on the elevator together at
the end of a hot, sticky day. The
younger man was completely done
in, and he noted with surprise that
his senior was fresh as a daisy.

"I don't understand," he marveled,
"how you can listen to patients
from nine to five on a day like this
and still look so cheerful when
it's over."

The older analyst said simply,
"Who listens?"

— *Anonymous*

STOP me if you've heard this one...
ED FISCHER

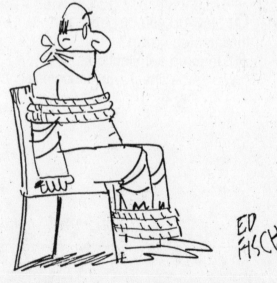

Anybody who has ever used the expression, "It was no Sunday School picnic" has obviously never been to a Sunday School picnic.

–The Parish Chute

~~

There are two ways a sermon can help: Some rise from a sermon greatly strengthened, others wake up greatly refreshed.

– The Joyful Noiseletter

~~

Q: How do you disperse a threatening crowd?
A: Take up a collection.

– The Joyful Noiseletter

Could you keep it down a little?
ED FISCHER

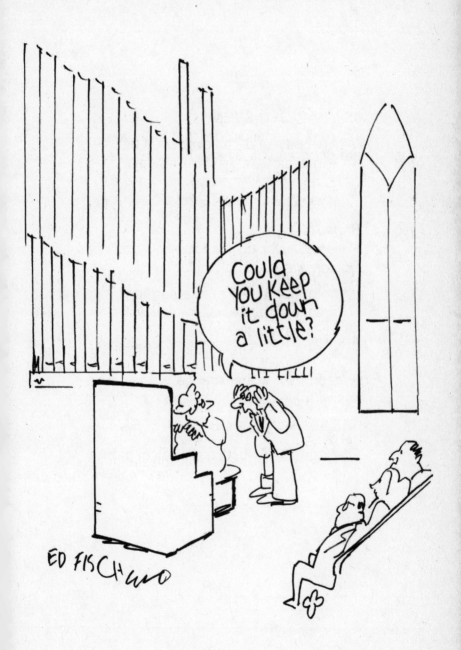

85-YEAR-OLD SVEN:
There is scientific proof that birthdays
are good for you. The more you have,
the longer you live.

~~

Sick Jokes...
Patient: Doctor, doctor, I swallowed a bone.
Doctor: Are you choking?
Patient: No, I'm serious.

~~

Al's wife: It's strange. Joe fell off a 20-foot
ladder and was in bed for a week.
A friend: Why is that strange?
Al's wife: He fell off the bottom rung.

~~

After age 70, it's just patch, patch, patch.
— *Jimmy Stewart*

1
I know how you feel...
2
BONK!
3
NOW you know how I feel.
ED FISCHER

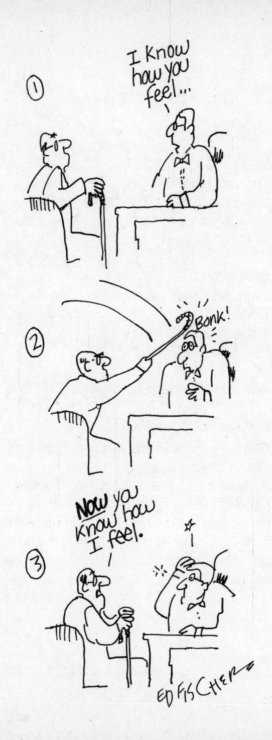

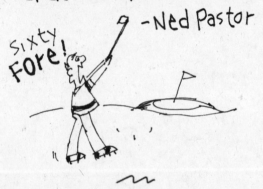

Now that I am
Sixty-Nine but not
quite yet a sage,
I just have one
ambition left, and
that's to shoot my age.

— Ned Pastor

At my age I have trouble remembering all the official rules. So, I keep it simple. If I lose a ball I add a stroke. If I find a ball I deduct a stroke. I often play with my dog, a golden retriever, and hit twenty or thirty under par. People ask me what my handicap is. I reply: "With or without my dog?"

— Bruce Lansky

1
Great!! We're behind this slow, old fart!
2
BOP!
3
FORE!
ED FISCHER

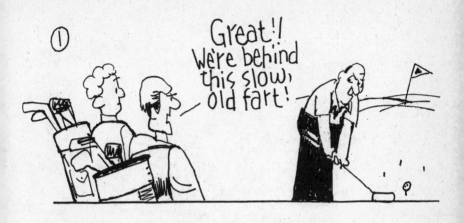

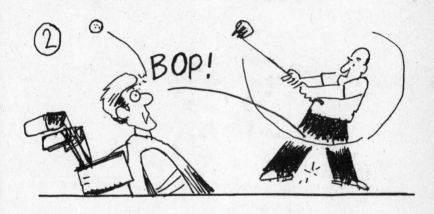

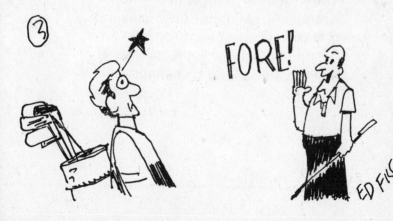

There's nothing wrong
with the younger generation
that becoming taxpayers
won't cure.
                    —Thomas LaMance

My father worked for the same firm
for twelve years. They fired him.
They replaced him with a tiny
gadget this big. It does everything
that my father does, only much
better. The depressing thing is—my
mother ran out and bought one.
                    – Woody Allen

Here's your problem, Grandpa- you forgot to turn it on...
ED FISCHER

Q: Why don't retired nurses like to give toasts?
A: They're tired of saying "bottoms up."

Q: What's the most important key to a successful retirement?
A: Don't die on the job.

Q: What's the biggest advantage of retiring at age sixty-two?
A: Not working at age sixty-three.

Q: What do you call a retired boss?
A: Anything you want.

Q: Why does a retiree often say he doesn't miss the job but he misses the people he used to work with?
A: He's too polite to tell the whole truth.

— *Bill Dodds*

You gave up golf for this!?
ED FISCHER

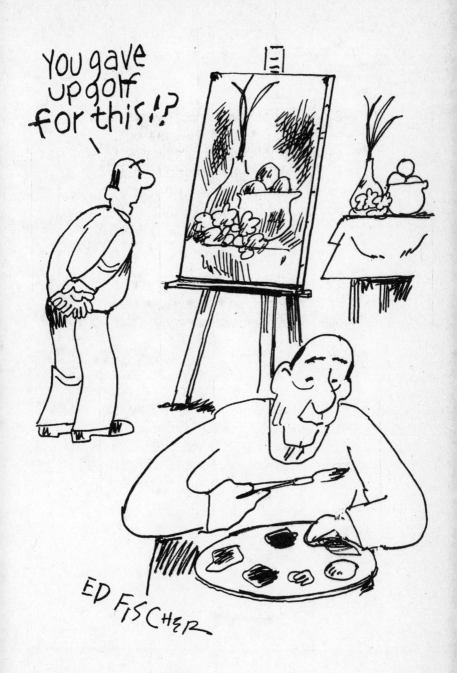

Did you ever see the customers in health-food stores? They are pale, skinny people who look half dead. In a steak house, you see robust, ruddy people. They're dying, of course, but they look terrific.

— *Bill Cosby*

I told my doctor I get very tired when I go on a diet, so he gave me pep pills. Know what happened?
I ate faster.

— *Joe E. Lewis*

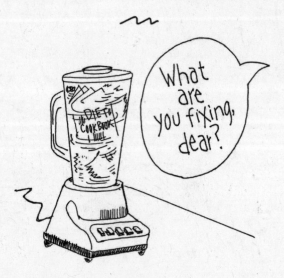

Does this mean you're off your diet?
ED FISCHER

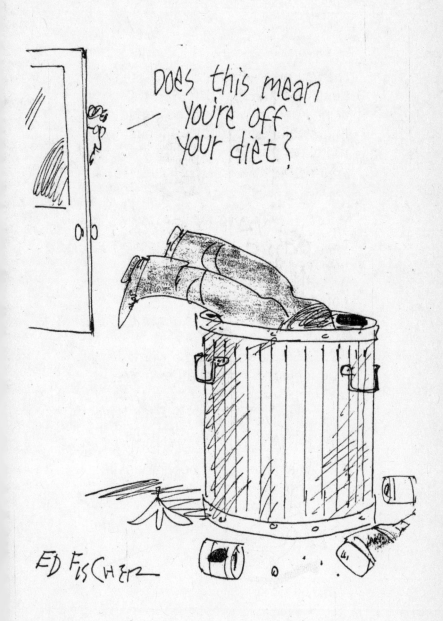

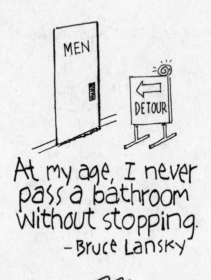

At my age, I never pass a bathroom without stopping.
– Bruce Lansky

〜

Q: Is 50 too young to be worried about bladder control problems?
A: Depends.

– P. D. Witte

〜

Q: What is the most popular destination for 60-year-old air travelers?
A: The airplane bathroom.

– P. D. Witte

Guess we should stop more often.
REST ROOMS
seniors country TOURS
ED FISCHER

Psychiatrist to his
nurse: Just say
we're very busy... Don't
keep saying it's a
madhouse.
        —Anonymous

∿

My first psychiatrist said I was paranoid,
but I want to get a second opinion
because I think he's out to get me.
        — *Tom Wilson ("Ziggy")*

∿

After twelve years of therapy my
psychiatrist said something that
brought tears to my eyes. He said,
"No hablo inglès."
        — *Ronnie Shakes*

Z Z Z z
Z Z Z z
ED FISCHER

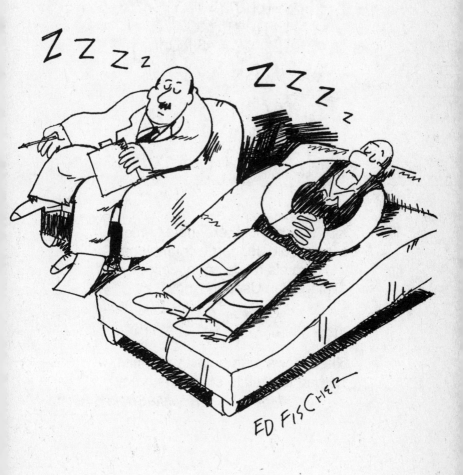

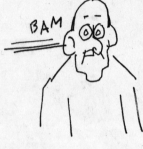

Don't worry about senility—
My grandfather used to
say—when it hits you,
you won't know it.
—Bill Cosby

Q: Why aren't there more
50-year-old Jeopardy champions?
A: There's no category called
"Things You Used to Know."
— *P. D. Witte*

The older a man gets, the farther
he had to walk to school as a boy.
— *Anonymous*

MAP 1 2 3 4 5
A
B
C
D
E
from your loving spouse
Where your stuff is...
under wear
X←You are here
cuff links
socks
shirts
Your socks are at D-5.
ED FISCHER

Growing old has one
advantage. You'll
never have to do
it again.

~~

One must wait until the evening to
see how splendid the day has been.
— *Sophocles*
(on old age)

~~

We do not remember days;
we remember moments.
— *Cesare Pavese*

~~

As long as you're over the hill, you
might as well enjoy the view.
— *Anonymous*

THE ROAD
LESS
TRAVELED
ED FISCHER

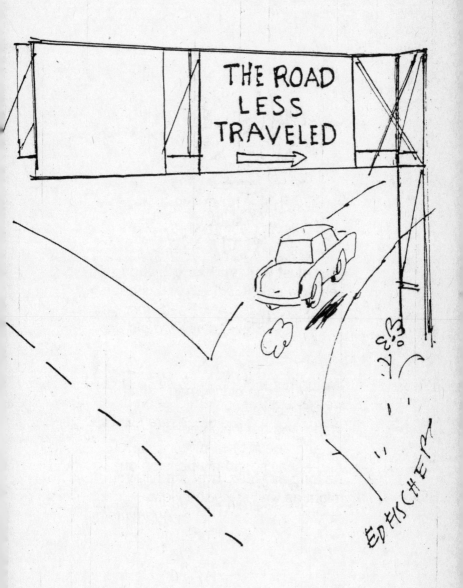

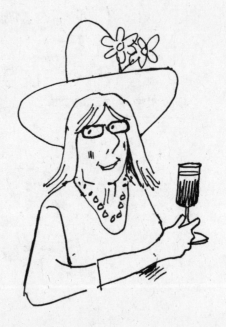

When I am an old woman I shall
  wear purple.
With a red hat which doesn't go,
  and doesn't suit me.
And I shall spend my pension on
  brandy and summer gloves...
  – *"Warning" by Jenny Joseph*